The Celts

AND ALL THAT

For Karl

The Celts

AND ALL THAT

Allan Burnett

Illustrated by
Scoular Anderson

First published in 2016 by
Birlinn Limited
West Newington House
10 Newington Road
Edinburgh
EH9 1QS

www.bcbooksforkids.co.uk

ISBN: 978 1 78027 392 1

British Library Cataloguing-in-Publication Data
A catalogue record for this book is available from the British Library

Designed by James Hutcheson

Page make up by Mark Blackadder

Printed and bound by Grafica Veneta SpA
(www.graficaveneta.com)

Contents

Prologue

Prologue

It was late spring of 685 AD – more than thirteen centuries ago.

A warrior king called Ecgfrith was marching north through the wooded and snow-capped mountains of northern Britain when he and his men came upon a fortress by a lake.

The forty-year-old Ecgfrith held up his hand to call a halt and the jangling of the men's weapons and packs suddenly stopped. Only the swishing tails of the cavalry horses kept moving.

Ecgfrith looked around the shores of the lake. Hiding in the fortress, or somewhere in the surrounding forest, was his enemy – a tribe of Celts.

'Come out, come out, you cowardly Celts!' shouted Ecgfrith, his voice booming across the lake, through the trees and around the mountains.

A pair of swallows screamed overhead, causing some of Ecgfrith's men and horses to twitch nervously. But of the Celts there was no sign.

The Celts were hiding, but not out of fear. They just wanted Ecgfrith to *think* they were afraid.

This was all the plan of the Celts' leader – King Bridei.

Bridei and his cunning Celts had fooled Ecgfrith by pretending to retreat into the hills while Ecgfrith's army advanced from the south.

Now they had Ecgfrith right where they wanted him. It was a trap, and Ecgfrith had just marched right into it.

With swords and spears at the ready, Bridei and his band of warriors began creeping out of the forest. Others, who had been hiding in the fortress, took aim with their bows and arrows. Ecgfrith and his men were about to be ambushed.

Ecgfrith, with his eyes screwed shut and hands cupped over his mouth, bellowed once more.

'Come out, come out . . .' he began, expecting the cowering Celts to appear with their hands up, ready to be taken prisoner.

But one of Ecgfrith's warriors tapped his shoulder. 'Errr, I think they've come out, sire.'

Ecgfrith looked around. He and his men had been surrounded. This was not part of the plan.

'Now then,' Ecgfrith began again with a nervous cough, trying to hide his terror, 'if you agree to come quietly . . .'

But this time he was cut short. A Celtic arrow whizzed through the air and speared a man on horseback next to him. The wide-eyed warrior groaned as he slumped forwards in his saddle and then fell onto the moor with a thud.

Now the Celts suddenly rushed forward!

More arrows flew through the air, accompanied by spears and rocks. To Ecgfrith's left and right, his men were skewered like wild boar ready for roasting.

Swords were drawn from Celtic scabbards and thrust into the invaders' bellies with a squelch. Horses trampled on the wounded and the dying.

Heads were cut off and taken as trophies by some especially bloodthirsty Celts who liked doing things the old-fashioned way.

Ecgfrith's men fought back, but to no avail.

Amid it all, Ecgfrith was slain. At the end of the battle he lay in a bloody heap on the moor by the lake, next to the bodies of his men.

It was a thumping victory for the Celts, and a great day

for King Bridei, whose heroism would be remembered for generations to come.

But it was a dreadful day for Ecgfrith's tribe, who were known as the Angles.

The Angles had originally come to Britain across the North Sea from Jutland, which is now part of Denmark and northern Germany. They settled in Northumbria, in the country later known as England.

They had been trying to expand their territory northwards, but the Celts were having none of it. The thing is, once upon a time the Celts had lived throughout the length and breadth of Britain – and much of Europe, too. They were fed up of being squeezed by invaders and were determined to fight for their survival.

Perhaps Ecgfrith should have heeded those who warned him not to cross the Celts.

'I pleaded with him not to go,' said Ecgfrith's tearful spiritual adviser, Bishop Cuthbert.

'We would have told him not to go, too,' said the long-dead emperors of Rome, who had once built TWO walls to keep the barbarous northern Celts, also known as the Picts, out of Roman Britain.

'Go where?' said Bede, a famous medieval English monk and historian who later wrote about the ambush but had no idea where it actually happened.

Even today we are still unsure where exactly the battle took place. But at least we have a name for it. In fact, we have a couple.

To the celebrating Celts, the slaughter of poor old Ecgfrith became known as the Battle of Dun Nechtain. To the Angles it was the Battle of Nechtansmere.

It may have been fought at one of two places in the nation now called Scotland – at either Dunnichen in the Lowlands, or Dunachton in the Highlands. Since Dunachton is in a mountainous area, it might be the more likely location.

Where the battle took place is not the only sketchy detail. There's a lot about this battle that still has historians and archaeologists – experts who dig up the ground looking for clues – scratching their heads in doubt.

So the account you have just read is only a very rough and colourful idea of how things *might* have gone down on that day in 685. Other things we could speculate about include:

The answer to [C] is that they might have started off white, but likely turned brown after Ecgfrith was attacked by Bridei's men. But there are many more questions about this battle that we don't have an exact answer to.

The same is often true of all things Celtic. That's because the Celts can seem to be a mysterious, puzzling and shadowy people. Not much evidence about them survives.

Yet there is a lot about the Celts that we *do* know.

After all, they are one of the most colourful, exciting and talked-about people in history. Their adventures took them across seas and continents, and lasted for thousands of years.

In fact, the Celts helped create the world we live in today.

And that is why you must read on . . .

1

Who are the Celts?

The Celts have been around for thousands of years. During that time they have been known to eat strange food, wear strange clothes – or no clothes at all, which is even stranger – enjoy some *very* strange habits, and speak strange languages.

The details of all this strangeness will be revealed in the chapters that follow. As you read on, you should find it all becoming less strange and more familiar. Indeed, the ways of the ancient Celts may be a lot more familiar than you realise.

That's because the Celts are still with us today. In fact, you might even consider yourself to be one.

Try this quick Celt Test. Do you:

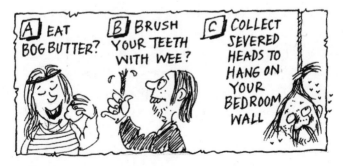

No, thought not. Or if you actually *do* do any of these things, you must be reading this book either in hospital or in a maximum-security prison.

We will return to the delights of bog butter, wee as toothpaste and severed heads later. But first we have to talk over a few basic facts about the Celts of today and the Celts of long ago.

To get started with this, let's turn back to our old friend Bridei. You know, the Celtic king you read about in the Prologue, who axed the Angles at the Battle of Dun Nechtain.

Bridei lived during the seventh century AD – that's between six and seven hundred years after the birth of Jesus Christ. Now, at that moment in time, the Celts had just gone through a pretty major turning point in their history.

About a thousand years before Bridei, the Celts were on the up. They lived in territories right across Europe, and were a wealthy and powerful force to be reckoned with.

For a while, the ancient Greeks and even the mighty Roman Empire cowered before them.

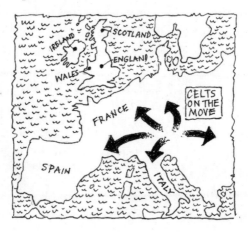

Then things changed. Celtic power crumbled, and they were forced to withdraw into the far north-western corner of the continent. They clung to the edge of France and the British Isles.

So instead of being on the up, the Celts went into a long decline. A real downer. This means that the heroic victory of Bridei was one of the last great Celtic success stories.

Speaking of Celtic heroes and their stories, you will encounter many more in this book – some real and some mythical. One of these heroes was King Arthur, who defended the Celts of Britain against all kinds of enemies.

Stories about such heroes as Arthur and Bridei helped keep the Celtic way of life alive as the centuries passed and the world moved on. So even though Celts today no longer have any really strange habits – well, maybe a few – they can still think of themselves as 'Celtic'.

Today the Celtic world has shrunk to just six Celtic nations. These are Brittany, Cornwall, Ireland, the Isle of Man, Scotland and Wales.

Some of these Celtic nations are part of larger modern nations, such as Brittany, which is part of France, and Cornwall, which is part of England. Mind you, there are still some Celts in both places who reckon Cornwall isn't English and Brittany isn't French.

Something that marks the Celtic nations out as different is their range of Celtic languages. Once upon a time these languages would have been spoken by many people. Now the number is far fewer.

In Brittany there is a language called Breton. In Cornwall there is Cornish. In Ireland they speak Gaelic. On the Isle of

Man there is Manx. Scotland has Scots Gaelic. And Wales – whose Celtic language today is the strongest – is the home of Cymraeg, or Welsh.

Language isn't everything though. After all, the language spoken by pretty much everyone throughout the British Isles and Ireland today is, of course, English.

In Scotland, there are also the remains of another old language – Scots. It is similar to English and partly comes from the old Danish language spoken by Ecgfrith and the Angles.

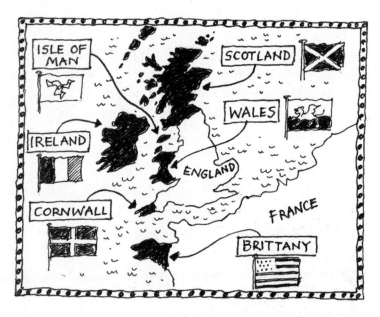

So what else makes a nation Celtic? Well, a lot of things, like art and music, traditions and ancestry… You'll find out more in the pages that follow.

So much for today's Celtic nations. But remember, there used to be Celts in many other places, too – and those other places will loom very large in this book.

Once upon a time, the whole of what is now England was Celtic. Among the greatest of all Celts was an English warrior princess called Boudicca. She was as tough as nails and you're going to love reading about her.

The Celtic world also included large parts of France, Austria, Spain and northern Italy, among other territories. Yet, as has already been mentioned, that was all a very long time ago.

Not so long ago, however, that we can't go back and take a closer look . . .

2

Back to the beginning

Now that we have uncovered some basic facts about the Celts, it's time to dig further. This requires us to burrow deep into the past, almost three thousand years ago, to the murky foundations of Celtic history. In other words, we are about to take a look at the very first Celts.

So what did the first Celts look like? Well, their clothing was a bit strange by today's standards. But in many ways they looked just like us.

Some ancient writers described the Celts as tall and strong with light hair. The also reported that Celtic men had long moustaches.

This is undoubtedly what some Celts looked like. For example, the skeleton of a six-foot-tall Celtic prince was recently discovered in a grave along with fantastically decorated treasures including a chariot, a couch and a cauldron.

In general, most Celts seem to have been about the same height as we are and many had dark hair.

Celtic girls and women wore dresses and skirts, with fur cloaks fastened by brooches. Their clothes were often finely woven from dyed wool and other fabrics to create patterns.

The Celts even used horsehair and badger fur to make things like belts and brushes. There was lots of jewellery too, including large gold bracelets worn on the wrist or around the neck.

Celtic boys and men wore shirts and trousers, with cloaks on top to keep them warm. Their cloaks were also fastened with brooches.

But remember, even during ancient Celtic times there were changing fashions, and people had individual styles. The Celts probably wore a wide variety of different clothes.

According to reports, in certain places and from time to time, some Celts dressed very strangely indeed – sometimes going completely naked except for tattoos painted all over their bodies.

Our ideas about what the Celts looked like come from ancient writing, but also from modern archaeologists – those experts who literally dig into the earth looking for history. Skeletons and bits of clothing have been found by archaeologists in graves and in peat bogs.

The bogs are cold, airless places with acidic soil, and this stops human remains from completely rotting away.

The places where Celtic bodies have been found also give us clues about where the early Celts actually lived.

Some of the first Celts seem to have lived in central Europe during the eighth century BC – that's at least seven hundred years Before Christ and more than 2,700 years before us. Their homeland was in the mountainous countries now known as Austria and Switzerland, and in territories nearby.

This part of Europe was an ideal place for people to flourish. It had fertile fields and long rivers, such as the Danube and the Rhine, which allowed local traders to sail across the continent to the seas beyond.

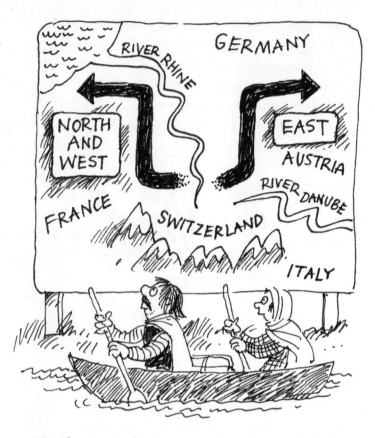

Now here's a really important fact: these early Celts also have two other names. Some of the earliest Celts are known as the Hallstatt people, and later Celts are known as the La Tène people. La Tène is pronounced 'Lah-ten'.

Details about the Hallstatt people are sketchy, but we know that they had a particular way of speaking, a particular way of designing artwork and tools, a particular kind of lifestyle, and so on. They may also have had a particular way of blowing their noses, but that's just a guess.

The Hallstatt way of life – or culture – gradually evolved into the La Tène culture, which was similar but different.

One of the important differences was the way the dead were buried. The chiefs of the later Hallstatt tribes of around 500 BC were buried with small hunting daggers, but the La Tène chiefs and warriors were buried with swords, spears and sometimes helmets.

It seems that weapons were needed by the La Tène folk because they were busy expanding their territory and fighting with neighbouring peoples.

The La Tène people also traded with tribes from further afield, including the Etruscans of northern Italy and the ancient Greeks.

This contact with outsiders gave the La Tène new ideas that turned them further away from the old Hallstatt way of life.

While all this was going on, the Hallstatt and La Tène people came to be known as Celts. Now, this is as good a time as any to point out that the words 'Celt' and 'Celtic' are rather a touchy subject. Historians and archaeologists argue endlessly about what a Celt actually is, or was, and whether such a people even existed at all. During these arguments, the history of the Celts sometimes seems to be buried under lots of complicated jargon …

Now, if you have Celtic ancestors, and this has got you worried that they might not have existed – which means that maybe *you* don't actually exist either – you can relax. The word 'Celt' is really just a word we use to try to make sense of a group of people who lived long ago.

The actual people did exist, of course. And many of them were definitely called 'Celts' – by themselves or by outsiders

– back in the day. *Keltoi* and *Galli* were two ancient Greek and Roman words which mean 'Celts'.

Now we've got that all cleared up, here's another important nugget of information to wrap your head around – the Celts were an Iron Age people.

So what does that mean, exactly?

The Iron Age sounds rather curious. It is not a name that the people who lived back then would ever have used themselves. It's another label that modern experts have written and then stuck onto the people of long ago to try to make sense of their lifestyles.

The Iron Age means a time when people began using iron metal instead of bronze metal to make tools, weapons and treasures. Bronze, which is harder to find and tougher to work with than iron, was used during the earlier Bronze Age. And the age before that was, you guessed it, the Stone Age.

The Celts are reckoned to be one of the first groups of people to learn how to make things with iron, and their iron goodies were sold or exchanged with other peoples around Europe.

Switching from the Bronze Age to the Iron Age was in some ways a big deal. Iron was a much more useful material than bronze. This means it was a big technological leap – like jumping off a horse and onto a motorbike, or throwing away pen and paper and tapping out an email, or blasting your dinner in a microwave instead of gently heating it in a pot on a stove.

On the other hand, life during the Iron Age carried on much as before. And bronze didn't disappear – people just made fewer bronze things than before.

By using iron, and by becoming better at using other metals, the Celts became more, well, Celtic. The blacksmiths and artists of the Celtic world created distinctively decorated swords, horse harnesses and treasures – all of which helped to give the Celts a sense of identity.

Something that has confused people for years is how exactly the early Celts, with their iron-making skills, first found their way from central Europe all the way over to the British Isles.

One theory is that the Celts were invaders or immigrants who moved to Britain and Ireland sometime between 800 and 500 BC.

Another theory is that it wasn't the Celtic people that invaded Britain. Instead, it was their ideas and their objects.

Celtic crockery, drinks and jewellery, for example, arrived in the British Isles on the boats of traders who sailed up and down Europe's Atlantic coast. Sea and river travel was an extremely useful and important way of getting about in those days.

In exchange for their goods, the traders bought from the Brits and Irish things like animals, grain, the ores needed to make metal, and even human slaves.

By embracing all that new Celtic stuff arriving on the boats – including new ideas and religious beliefs passed on by the traders – the local people of Britain and Ireland gradually became Celtic. The Celtic language, or languages, would have been spread or shared in this way too.

Just to confuse things, though, some experts take a very different view. They reckon that early 'Celtic' ideas, words and objects had already started appearing in Britain much earlier, during the Bronze Age.

But whether that happened thanks to traders, or because the people of Britain and Ireland came up with Celtic ideas of their own, or because a bunch of Celtic people invaded from the continent, is hard to say. A combination of all three is possible.

Luckily, we can say for sure that there were times when Celtic people definitely did move from place to place in large numbers. And when they went looking for a fight, things got really interesting . . .

3

Brennus the menace

Around 390 BC, a Celtic tribe called the Senones went on the warpath in Italy. Their leader was called Brennus – a lean, mean fighting machine.

News of the advancing Celtic army caused panic. In the countryside, farmers fled in terror. In the cities, the townsfolk barricaded themselves in and took up their weapons.

Having already moved into the very north of the country, the Celts were heading south in search of glory and riches.

After years of trade with wealthy Italian tribes, such as the Etruscans, the Celts knew Italy was full of goodies such as wine, olive oil, figs, fine clothes, artworks and treasure. Now the Celts had a brainwave: *let's just clobber them and steal their stuff.*

On the way south the Celts attacked the Etruscan town of Clusium, which nowadays is part of Tuscany. But their final destination was a much bigger prize.

As Brennus and his warriors marched along, they let everyone know their sights were set on the great city of Rome.

About eleven miles north of Rome, Brennus called a halt on a wide plain where the River Allia flowed down from the mountains into another river – the Tiber.

Brennus could see a Roman army marching towards them from the south. Having heard of the Celts' advance, the Romans had hastened there to try to prevent an attack on their beloved city.

The stage was set for one of the first great battles between the Celts and the Romans. The details of what happened are unclear, and there is more than one version of events. Even the year is uncertain, though we know the date was 18 July.

Anyway, the battle went something like this ...

THE ARMIES HAD A FEW THOUSAND MEN EACH — ON FOOT AND HORSEBACK.

THE ROMANS SPREAD OUT IN A THIN LINE TO STOP THE CELTS FROM GETTING ROUND THEIR FLANKS TO ATTACK FROM BEHIND.

ROMANS

TO THE FLANKS

CELTS

Suddenly, with a raging battle cry, Brennus charged his men uphill towards the Roman army's right side. But instead of standing their ground, the terrified Romans just turned and ran.

This move caused panic, and soon the whole lot tried to make a run for it. As the Romans pushed against each other,

trying to escape, many were accidentally stabbed or speared in the back by their own side.

Anyone the Celts caught up with was hacked, slashed, skewered and splattered. According to some reports, the Celts later spent hours cutting off heads and collecting them as trophies.

Meanwhile, the remaining Romans tried to get away by swimming across the River Tiber. Some were dragged under its swirling waters by the weight of their armour and drowned. Others were hit by the hail of spears that the Celts threw into the river. But many of those smart enough to dump their armour and weapons did manage to swim to the opposite bank and stagger away.

And that was the Battle of the Allia – a humiliating defeat for the Romans, who had simply not been up to the job. It was an easy victory for the Celts – perhaps too easy.

In fact, Brennus reckoned the Romans were luring him into some kind of trap. His suspicions were confirmed when his scouts reported that the city gates of Rome were still open.

So Brennus decided to wait a while. He camped outside the city while his men celebrated their victory and showed off the booty plundered from the battlefield.

When he was sure the coast was clear, Brennus entered the gates of Rome. Once inside, the Celts were met by an eerie sight.

Instead of a garrison of defenders, the Celts found a series of frighteningly lifelike statues of men in robes, sitting in the porches of grand houses.

One curious Celt reached out to touch the face of one of the statues. But when the Celt tugged at the statue's beard, it suddenly leapt up and struck him on the head with its staff.

These were no statues! They were real Roman senators, who had been giving the invaders the silent treatment. The Celts were enraged. They slaughtered the senators then went on a rampage.

Meanwhile, a small force of young Romans had assembled in a fortress inside the city called the Capitoline Hill. While other survivors fled, these warriors became Rome's last bastion of defence.

A group of Celts raised their shields over their heads and tried to march up the hill to take the citadel – but they were pushed back under a hail of spears and rocks.

Eventually, after blockading the Romans for ages to try to starve them into submission, Brennus learned about a secret route up the cliffs to the top of the hill and ordered a surprise attack.

A small band of Celts silently climbed up during the night, managing to elude the guards and guard dogs at the top of the hill.

But the Celts' footsteps were heard by a gaggle of geese, who began cackling and beating their wings to alert the guards.

The leader of the guards was called Marcus Manlius. With a lunge of his heavy shield he smashed the face of one Celt, who went tumbling down the hill, taking others with him. The remaining Celtic raiders were speared, beaten or flung off the cliff at the top of the hill.

But Brennus wasn't too bothered. The rest of his army had brought the city to its knees. Eventually, the Romans were forced to cave in – which was just as well because the Celts were by now sick and starving too.

A ransom was paid so that Brennus would leave Rome in peace. The Romans agreed to hand over gold pieces weighing a thousand pounds (1,000 lbs) – about the weight of a horse.

The Romans accused the Celts of overloading the weighing scales, forcing them to hand over too much gold.

On hearing the Romans complain, Brennus unbuckled his iron sword and threw that on the scales too, meaning even more gold was required.

Then Brennus turned to the Romans and roared, 'Woe to the vanquished!' Which is another way of saying, 'Look, you lost – now hand over the loot!'

Eventually, however, Brennus and his army got their comeuppance. According to some reports they were destroyed in battle by an army of Roman reinforcements. Others say they met their doom further north, while marching home.

There must have been something especially menacing about the name Brennus, because about a century later another Brennus led a huge Celtic army of about 40,000 men south-east through an area known as the Balkans to attack ancient Greece.

This happened in 279 BC, after the death of the great Balkan war leader Alexander the Great of Macedonia. Alexander's death left the area vulnerable to attack and Brennus took his chance.

The Celts thundered through Greece to the foot of the mighty Greek mountain of Parnassus. On the side of the mountain was the sacred Temple of Delphi, which contained a hoard of treasure. Brennus ordered them to grab the lot.

During the siege of the lofty temple, the Celts must have upset the Greek gods. The raiders were blasted by snowstorms and battered by falling rocks from the mountain. The mortal Greeks fought back, too, and Brennus was wounded – forcing the Celts to retreat northwards.

Shamed by his failure, Brennus committed suicide. The remains of his army joined other Celts to head further east into Asia Minor, which today is the nation called Turkey.

The stories of the two bad boys called Brennus are legendary – which means some parts may or may not be true. A lot of what we know comes from Roman and Greek writers who were prone to exaggeration, or even making things up. But the bare bones are probably pretty accurate.

What we do know is that the Celts were keen to expand their territory. Some say this was because their original homelands were overcrowded. Others suggest the Celts were trying to build an empire. A third way of looking at it is that the Celts were mostly a peaceful and civilised folk, but a few loved to plunder and pillage.

One thing's for sure, the weapons the Celts used to make their mark in new lands were awesome. So let's take a closer look . . .

4

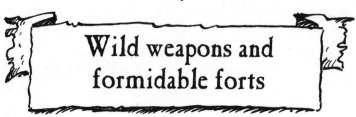

Wild weapons and formidable forts

Now that you've had a taste of what the ancient Celts were like in battle, it's time to take a closer look at their weaponry. Just don't get *too* close, unless you want to lose an arm or a leg.

Staying out of harm's way is easier said than done, though. If a battle-hardened Celtic warrior were to come screaming towards you, chances are he would be swinging a terrifyingly long, terrifyingly heavy and terrifyingly sharp sword.

It might be best to just shut your eyes and wait for one of the following sounds:

The long sword left the person wielding it vulnerable to a cunning counterattack with a short sword at very close range, but it was still a classic Celtic weapon – and boy did it cause carnage.

Good ones were expensive to make and often beautifully decorated at the hilt – which is the handle – with human-like figures.

If used properly, the long sword wasn't just a weapon of attack. It also acted as a shield. By swinging the sword around him or her, an expert Celtic warrior created a space into which nobody but the most experienced opponent would dare to step. That's unless they wanted to carry bits of themselves home in a basket.

An enemy warrior carrying a spear, for example, would have to lunge dangerously close to have any chance of striking. And if they missed, the swinging blade would make them wish they hadn't bothered.

That's not to say the spear was useless – far from it. If you managed to hit the target while using a spear, the wound was more likely to kill an opponent than a blow from a sword.

Spears were a very popular Celtic weapon and generally came in two varieties. There was the short spear, and the long spear.

The short spear was like a javelin: you threw it at the enemy. So it was handy to have a few of them in a bag slung over your shoulder. Once you had run out of spears, you would close in on the enemy and draw your sword for hand-to-hand combat.

The long spear, which was about the same height as a man, was used like a lance – you held it in your hands and thrust it at your opponent. Even if you missed, you could still do some damage by ripping your opponent's flesh with the broad, sharp tip as you pulled the spear back.

The tip of the spear used only a small amount of metal, which meant spears were cheaper and easier to make than swords. With its thick wooden shaft, a long spear could also be used to block the blows of an opponent's sword.

Just as a spear or sword could be used as a shield, then there were also times when a shield could be used as a weapon. Celtic shields were made of wood, and often covered with leather and reinforced with metal.

Shields came in many shapes and sizes, including round and hexagonal, and were often highly decorated. Usually they were oval or rectangular and had a thick section known as a boss in the centre to protect the wearer's hand.

THE SHIELD SHOP.

Mounted on the inside of the boss was a handle, which allowed the wearer to thrust the shield at the enemy and make him tumble backwards.

You could also thrust your shield to jam the enemy's arm and prevent him from using his sword. A really big shield was handy for blocking the enemy's view while you neatly slashed at his ankles.

Other Celtic weapons included the dagger and the sling, which was a length of cord with a pouch attached to it for slinging a missile at the enemy. The choice of missile could include:

A	A ROCK	
B	A METAL BALL	
C	SHEEP DROPPINGS	

Choosing C might sound tempting if you wanted to be really nasty, but a poo pellet would cause virtually no harm. So sling-shooters mostly went for rocks, or metal pieces if they were available. A sling was cheap and easy to make, but it took practice to make sure you hit the right target.

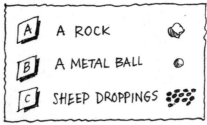

You really don't know how to use this, do you?

URK!

42

If you found yourself on the receiving end of a sling, a blade or a thrusting shield then it was a good idea to be well protected. A thick leather jacket called a jerkin would shield your body a bit, as would wearing a wide band of bronze or gold, known as a torc, around your neck.

Wealthy warriors could afford metal armour, and Celtic blacksmiths invented a famous kind known as chain mail.

However, most Celtic warriors had no armour at all, and went into battle wearing their usual clothes, such as a shirt, patterned trousers and a cloak. Then there were those who are thought to have rushed at the enemy wearing nothing at all – except perhaps for tattoos or a blue skin dye called woad, with a substance called lime in their hair to make it white and spiky.

Often Celtic warriors would go bare-chested with just a pair of trousers on – and if they wanted to look really scary, they would dangle the severed heads of their previous conquests from their belt.

CHAIN MAIL

TORC

LEATHER JERKIN

In general, the Celts liked to look and sound as threatening as possible on the battlefield. For this, they also used the following equipment and techniques:

A Their helmets sometimes had terrifying metal decorations on them – such as horns, or ravens with hinged wings that flapped when the wearer moved.

B They chanted and roared as aggressively as possible, and blew frighteningly loud bronze war horns. One such horn was the carnyx, an upright trumpet decorated with a fierce animal head on the end of a long stem, which was held above the player's head.

C They sometimes rode thundering horse-drawn chariots on two or four wheels. These vehicles terrified any enemy in their path and allowed elite warriors to get dropped off on

the front line and then picked up later if they got into trouble.

What all this means, in short, is that when the Celts went to war they didn't muck about. The same goes for their attitude towards protecting their own homes from attack.

Often the Celts' enemies were foreigners such as the Romans or Greeks, but frequently the enemy would be a neighbouring tribe of Celts. This made it important to have fortresses and villages that were safe and secure.

Hill forts were the answer, and from earliest times the Celts built a lot of them. The largest were like small towns.

There were many different ways to build a hill fort. Here is a classic method:

This method of construction is known as a 'Gallic wall'. The word Gallic refers to a place known as Gaul, which if it existed today would be in France and parts of its surrounding countries. The people of Gaul were known as Gauls – which is another word for Celts.

Inside the walls, the Gauls went about their business. Blacksmiths, leather workers and carpenters made swords, armour, shields and spears. Others baked bread or prepared meat. Still others cleaned or made clothes.

All the while people came and went, hugging, arguing, laughing, crying, singing or being silent and picking their noses when they thought nobody else was looking. A lot like today, really.

When under attack, the hill fort could be defended by warriors standing on top of the wall and using slings, arrows and spears.

It was just as well that the hill forts of Gaul were strong and well defended, because during the first century BC, the Celts who lived in them were attacked by a mighty empire . . .

5

Romans and Gauls

Imagine a Celtic hill fort somewhere in Gaul during the first century BC. The tribe living there have gathered around a log fire to listen to a story …

53

This imaginary scene tells us a key historical fact: the Roman invasion of Gaul had begun. The Romans were no longer content just living in their corner of Italy. They were building an empire that one day would span the length and breadth of Europe.

Gaul was a troublesome yet juicy slice of territory that the Romans were itching to sink their teeth into. In fact, they had been preparing their takeover of Gaul for generations.

At first the Romans used the softly-softly approach. Roman traders travelled around Gaul selling goodies such as wine, olives and fine pottery in return for meat and even human slaves.

But this tempted the Celts of Gaul to attack wealthy Roman trading posts, such as the great walled city of Massilia by the Mediterranean Sea.

So then the Romans got tough. In 125 BC the people of Massilia – who were originally from Greece – asked the Roman army to help them get rid of the Celtic raiders. The Celts were driven back from Massilia and the Romans set up a fort nearby to police the area.

To make it clear to everyone that they were now in charge, the Romans included this area in a new province – or territory – they set up in 121 BC. It was called Transalpine Gaul.

The name 'Transalpine Gaul' meant the part of Gaul on the far side of the Alps from Rome. Roughly speaking, the heartland of Transalpine Gaul lay across southern France. Massilia is now the city of Marseilles.

About a century earlier, the Romans had conquered another province they called 'Cisalpine Gaul', which you can

LAND OF THE CELTIC GAULS 'LONG HAIRS'

MOUNTAINS OF THE ALPS

TRANSALPINE GAUL

CISALPINE GAUL

MASSILIA

ROME

also see on the map above. This was the part of Gaul on the near side of the Alps – in other words, nearest to Rome.

Today, Cisalpine Gaul would be roughly northern Italy. Here the Romans took their revenge on the Celts for attacking them back in the days of Brennus.

So far so good for the Romans. The trouble was that the Celts of Gaul – also known simply as the Gauls – still lived freely over most of what is now France and Belgium.

This large area was known as 'Long-haired Gaul', so called because the Romans reckoned the Gauls there needed a haircut. Unless the Long-haired Gauls could be conquered, they would always be a threat to Roman territory.

So the Romans decided to get nasty. In fact, one Roman in particular decided to get nasty. His name was Julius Caesar, a cunning politician and skilled commander who was determined to bring all of Gaul under his control – and build a Roman Empire.

In 58 BC, Caesar became governor of the southern bits of Gaul that the Romans had already conquered. He immediately set out to try to crush the Celts in the rest of Gaul.

Caesar defeated a Celtic tribe called the Helvetii while they were fleeing through Gaul to try to get away from another enemy – the Germans. The surviving Helvetii tramped back to their original homeland to find the charred remains of their houses, which they had burned before leaving because they hadn't planned on going back. Oops.

The next year, Caesar marched his army further north. He battled a tribe of Gauls called the Belgae, who lived in what is now present-day Belgium. Although Caesar reckoned the Belgae were the fiercest Gauls, his army defeated them.

Caesar even attacked the Gauls at sea. In 56 BC he ordered his men to build a fleet of warships to attack the Veneti tribe who lived in Brittany – the western tip of Gaul that stuck out into the Atlantic Ocean.

Although the Veneti were expert sailors and their ships too strong to be rammed, the Romans came up with a cunning plan. They swept past the Veneti ships with hooks that cut the Veneti rigging and pulled down their sails.

Some Veneti tried to row away, but when it came to rowing the Romans were the masters. They caught up with the Veneti ships and jumped aboard. Though a few got away, many Veneti sailors were killed or captured.

More battles followed. The Romans were often outnumbered yet they still managed to beat the Gauls. There were two reasons for this:

A. The Roman army had better weapons and fighting techniques.

B. The tribes of Gaul often fought among themselves, making it easy to pick them off one by one.

Eventually, the Gauls realised they needed to work together or their homeland would be lost. So they called a meeting.

In January 52 BC, representatives from tribes far and wide met in secret to discuss what to do. The conversation might have gone something like this:

Whatever the actual discussion beforehand, we know the basic facts of what happened next.

A strike team of warriors from a tribe called the Carnutes in central Gaul got dressed up as friendly merchants and went into their own capital city of Cenabum.

After dark, the Gauls crept into the houses where Roman settlers were spending the night. The Gauls took out their swords and murdered the sleeping Romans.

After this shocking success, many more Gauls became eager to put tribal differences aside and rebel against Rome. One of them was a young nobleman called Vercingetorix.

Vercingetorix – let's call him Getorix for short – was a member of the Arverni tribe. He was brave, ambitious and eager to be a great leader.

Getorix set out on his horse to visit the forts, farms and villages of different tribes with a simple message . . .

Soon, thousands of warriors were gathered around Getorix. At last, the Gauls had an army strong enough to take on the Romans in a big battle. This army began harassing those Gauls who still sided with Rome, and threatened Roman settlers.

When Caesar found out, he was enraged. His army went on the rampage, slaughtering thousands of villagers. But Getorix fought back. Both sides lost many warriors.

Eventually there was a showdown. Getorix pulled his men back to the hill fort of Alesia. The plan was to lure the Romans into besieging the fort and tire them out – just in time for Gaulish reinforcements to arrive.

But Caesar fought off the Gauls' reinforcements, leaving Getorix and his men stranded. Getorix realised all was lost. Some reports say he went to Caesar and threw down his weapons and armour. Transported to Rome in chains, Getorix was held prisoner for six years. He was then strangled at a party to celebrate the greatness of Caesar.

Gaul was now completely conquered. The Gauls did not disappear, but under Roman rule they became less Celtic and more Roman. Yet, the Celts continued to thrive in other lands. Before we find out what was in store for them, it's time to delve deeper into the Celtic way of life . . .

6

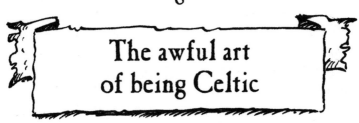

The awful art of being Celtic

This might sound hard to believe, but most of the time the ancient Celts were a civilised and peaceful bunch. They liked to play games. They loved to sing and dance. They adored listening to music, admiring works of art and wearing fashionable clothes.

The Celts grew beautiful things, invented clever things, wrote mysterious things, discovered amazing things and hunted for wild things. But they also ate and drank some rather DISGUSTING things.

'Oh? *How* disgusting?' you may ask. Well, what's the most awful thing you have ever eaten? Is it . . .

A Onion-flavoured ice cream?

B A snot sandwich?

C Bog butter?

If the answer is 'none of the above', then who can blame you? The first one sounds pretty vile. Although you probably suspect at least one of your weirder friends has tried the second one.

But surely no one would dare to even think about opening their mouths, sticking out their tongue and tasting bog butter!

Unless they were a hungry ancient Celt, that is.

So what is it, exactly? Well, the most disgusting kind of 'bog butter' was made by cutting the fat from a dead sheep or cow's kidneys, then grating it and cooking it until it melted. This oily fat was strained and cooled to make a substance called 'tallow'.

This could then be stuffed into the animal's bladder – hopefully it had been emptied and cleaned first! – before finally being buried in a peat bog for months or even years.

Sounds terrible, doesn't it? But it was actually a brilliant way of making sure no precious animal products went to waste, and the stuff was still edible after a year or more. Remember, peaty soil is great at preserving things.

Ah! Two years old! Delicious!

Bog butter was also made from milk in the

usual way, like real butter. This could be stored in a small wooden barrel – known as a keg – deep under the surface of the bog. These barrels of butter are still being discovered in Celtic lands to this day. The stuff does taste pretty dodgy after two thousand years, though.

Speaking of wooden barrels, according to the Romans these were a Celtic invention. The Celts used barrels to store one of their favourite drinks – beer.

But they didn't get too tipsy. Otherwise they would not have been able to come up with other great inventions, which included:

SOAP — MADE FROM ANIMAL FAT MIXED WITH ASH FROM THE FIRE.

BOARD GAMES — THE CELTS PLAYED ONE SIMILAR TO CHESS CALLED 'FIDCHELL'.

Gotcha!

MUSICAL INSTRUMENTS INCLUDED BONE FLUTES, BRONZE HAND BELLS AND STRINGED HARPS CALLED LYRES.

CALENDARS SOMETIMES MADE FROM SHEETS OF BRONZE, THEY DIVIDED THE YEAR INTO TWELVE MONTHS.

FARMING TOOLS SUCH AS THE IRON-TIPPED PLOUGH, MUCH BETTER THAN A WOODEN ONE.

By using good ploughs, the Celts were able to grow plenty of crops such as oats and barley. They flavoured their food with salt – which was also used to preserve food.

Salt was found by mining underground. Some Celtic mines were as deep as two hundred metres! Another method was to heat seawater in a pan over a fire, or using sunlight, until the water evaporated to leave just the salt.

A good dash of salt was added to many different Celtic recipes. One common Celtic dish, which could be made hot or cold, was gruel. This was a sort of porridge soup that included seeds, herbs and weeds.

Gruel could be pretty nasty depending on how it was made. Often it included meat, which would be butchered at the same time as making a bit of bog butter.

To get their hands on meat, of course, the Celts needed animals. There were two ways of getting meat from animals, fish and birds. These were hunting and farming.

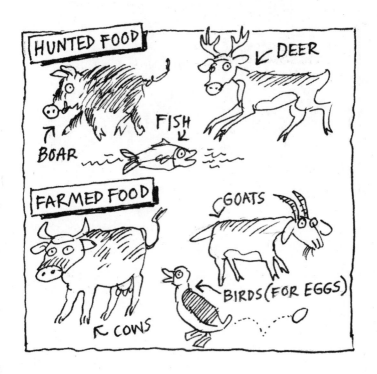

After all that farming, hunting, cooking and feasting, the Celts had to clean up. Out came the soap again, but also something truly terrifying: toothpaste made from urine.

Yes, that's right: some Celts brushed their teeth with *wee* as toothpaste. No wonder they went into battle in an absolute frenzy. They must have just brushed their teeth.

Does this information leave a bad taste in your mouth? Or perhaps that should be, your *gob*.

The word 'gob' – meaning mouth, or mouthful – is just one of many Celtic words that have found their way into the English language. Here are a few more:

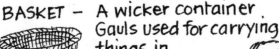
CELTIC DICTIONARY
POCKET EDITION

BASKET — A wicker container. Gauls used for carrying things in

BARD — A story-teller or poet

BANSHEE — A wailing fairy from Ireland

BROGUES — Sturdy shoes

CAIRN — A pile of stones

CAR — Once a chariot or cart, today, a motor vehicle

CLOCK — Irish word for bell

CORGI — Welsh word for small dog

DAD — From the Welsh 'tad'

FLANNEL — A useful piece of cloth

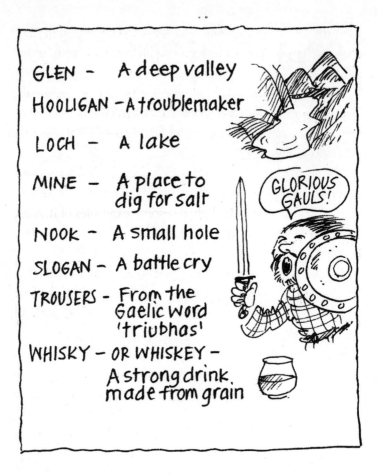

GLEN – A deep valley

HOOLIGAN – A troublemaker

LOCH – A lake

MINE – A place to dig for salt

NOOK – A small hole

SLOGAN – A battle cry

TROUSERS – From the Gaelic word 'triubhas'

WHISKY – OR WHISKEY – A strong drink made from grain

GLORIOUS GAULS!

These words come from different Celtic languages. Some of those languages are still around – such as Welsh and Gaelic. Others have become extinct, such as Gaulish.

Still, Gaulish hasn't vanished *completely*. It has been found written down on sheets of metal and chiselled into slabs of stone.

The Celts also chiselled amazing artwork into stone using

patterns of circles, spirals and leaves. These designs are enough to make you feel hypnotised if you look at them for long enough.

Another favourite subject for Celtic art was animals. Horses, for example, were a popular design on gold and silver Celtic coins. The Celts used coins to buy and sell things just as we do today.

The good news about all this Celtic art, coins, recipes and other bits and pieces is that you don't have to travel back in time to find some particularly awesome examples of it. A lot still survives in museums and galleries – and more may even be lying undiscovered in a field near your house.

The bad news is that there used to be much more of it around. After the Celts of Gaul were conquered, the last remaining Celts were nearly destroyed too – along with all their treasures.

Yep, blame those blasted Romans again . . .

7

Battles of Britain

In a remote corner of Europe, the Celts continued to go about their business safe from the wretched Romans. Since we are about to discover what happened when the Romans *did* turn up, though, we should perhaps turn our Celtic calendar back a bit first and learn more about this mysterious place.

We can start by looking up the long-lost travel log of an ancient mariner called Pytheas. Around 330 BC, Pytheas and his crew left Massilia on Gaul's south coast, seeking adventures in uncharted territory. This is what they discovered:

THE ACTUAL WRITINGS OF PYTHEAS HAVE DISAPPEARED BUT WE KNOW HIS REPORTS CONTAINED A LOT OF USEFUL INFORMATION.

We sailed through the PILLARS OF HERCULES at GIBRALTAR into the ATLANTIC OCEAN.

ATLANTIC OCEAN

BRETTANIKE

GAUL

SPAIN

ITALY

GIBRALTAR

We turned north and came to a group of cold and mysterious islands which were full of <u>CELTS</u>. These CELTS are a lot like the <u>GAULS</u> and have many of the same awful habits.

One of these islands is enormous. I think the locals call it <u>YNYSPRYDEIN</u> or <u>PRYDEINIKE</u> or something like that. I'm going to call the place BRETTANIKE which is something similar.

Brettanike today is known as Great Britain. Pytheas also sailed around neighbouring islands, including Ireland, the Isle of Man, and the Western and Northern Isles of Scotland. He probably set foot on a few of them, and would have found them teeming with people. As we discovered in chapter two, the Celts had probably been living in the British Isles and Ireland for a very long time.

Pytheas definitely went ashore at Cornwall in south-west Britain. He saw how the Celts there mined for tin metal, which was transported by merchants over to Gaul to make weapons and jewellery.

Pytheas also noted that people lived in thatched houses. Over the centuries, the thatched houses of Celtic Britain and Ireland were built in different shapes and sizes.

1 ROUNDHOUSES

THATCHED ROOF

NO CHIMNEY. SMOKE FROM FIREPLACE DRIFTED OUT THROUGH ROOF

WALLS OF STONES OR WOODEN POSTS

2 BROCHS OR DUNS

STRONG STONE FORTRESS INVENTED BY SCOTTISH CELTS. DOUBLE WALL WITH PASSAGES AND STAIRWAY BETWEEN.

3 WHEELHOUSES

FOUND MOSTLY IN SCOTLAND—HEBRIDEAN AND NORTHERN ISLES.
THEY WERE OFTEN BUILT UNDERGROUND WITH ONLY THATCHED ROOF SHOWING. INDOOR WALLS WERE LIKE THE SPOKES OF A WHEEL WITH ROOMS IN BETWEEN.

4 CRANNOGS

HOUSES BUILT ON LOCHS ON ARTIFICIAL ISLANDS MADE OF STILTS OR STONE.
CRANNOGS POPULAR IN SCOTLAND AND IRELAND.

If these sturdy and cosy houses are anything to go by, life in Celtic Britain sounds like it was pretty good on the whole.

What could possibly go wrong? Oh wait . . . We nearly forgot about the Romans.

The Roman leader Julius Caesar had crushed the Celtic Gauls.

Now he had his eyes on the Celts of Britain …

THIS IS THE DIARY OF J. CAESAR

DATE: 55 BC. SAILED WITH A SMALL ARMY ACROSS THE SEA FROM GAUL. LANDED ON THE SOUTH COAST OF THE ISLAND CALLED BRITAIN. THE CELTS RUSHED AROUND IN CHARIOTS BUT WE THUMPED THEM. DIDN'T HANG AROUND AND WENT BACK TO GAUL

DEAD STORMY AT SEA!

Ta-ta!

I don't think we'll be seeing these Roman guys again!

DIARY OF J. CAESAR. TRIED ON NEW PAIR OF BOOTS. ATE A BIT OF CHEESE.

54 BC - BACK TO BRITAIN. TOOK 5 LEGIONS - 30,000 GOOD FIGHTING MEN. ALSO, A WAR ELEPHANT TO SCARE THE PANTS OFF THE CELTS. THUMPED THEM BUT NOT WORTH THE EFFORT SO WENT BACK HOME.

In return for being left alone, the British Celts agreed to trade with the Romans. The Celts must have hoped things would remain peaceful after that.

Unfortunately, the Romans had other ideas. In 43 AD, a massive new army was sent to Britain by Emperor Claudius.

Roman ships landed in Kent and dropped off soldiers who fought the Celts at the River Medway. The Celts were pushed back to the River Thames, where they were defeated. Those Celts who were not killed by swords or arrows ended up drowning in rivers or marshes trying to escape. The chiefs of eleven Celtic tribes then surrendered to the Romans.

One of the surviving Celtic leaders was called Caratacus. He refused to submit to the Romans and fled to Wales to organise a rebellion.

Caratacus inspired tribes such as the Silures and the Ordovices to rise up against Rome. As a result, Roman forts were destroyed and their legions took a battering. Eventually, however, Caratacus was defeated.

It now looked like the Celts of southern Britain were about to go the same way as the Gauls – flattened by the armies of Rome. But there was still a glimmer of hope.

In 60 AD, rebel tribes got together again for one last blast against the Romans. Their leader was an extraordinary warrior named Boudicca. She was brave, tough and armed to the teeth.

Boudicca was queen of the Iceni tribe in East Anglia and she had a lot of reasons for rebelling against the Romans.

My husband died leaving half his property to our daughters and half his property to the Roman Emperor to keep him sweet. But instead of being content with this generous deal, the Romans have punished us in the most brutal way...

...I have been whipped and beaten and my daughters attacked! I will not stand for this!!

Joined by other tribes, Boudicca and her warriors scored a series of spectacular successes against the Romans. They destroyed many Roman towns, which later had to be rebuilt.

Along the way, Boudicca and her band also destroyed the Roman Ninth Legion.

Boudicca was so successful because the main Roman army had been away in Wales, but it then returned east and Boudicca's rebels were forced to do battle. Where exactly this showdown happened is a mystery, but we know it was probably somewhere in the English Midlands.

During the fight the Romans threw heavy spears, which stuck in the Celts' shields and weighed them down. Then the Romans closed in with their superior swords, armour and cavalry – who rushed at the Britons with long lances.

In the end the Roman army proved too powerful for the Celts and Boudicca's followers were massacred – including many children. It is said that the heartbroken Boudicca poisoned herself rather than submit to the Romans.

The Celts of southern Britain were now exhausted and submitted to living in peace under Roman rule. But Boudicca had blazed a trail for others to follow. There were still Celts around who were able to put up a fight. They lived in northern Britain – in the country we know today as Scotland.

The Romans knew these northern Celts would always be a threat unless they were dealt with. So in 79 AD the new Roman governor of Britain, Agricola, marched his legions of soldiers north through the mountain borderlands between England and Scotland, supported by a fleet of warships that sailed up the coast.

After defeating the English and Welsh Celts, the Romans might have thought the Scottish Celts would be a pushover. They were wrong.

The Celts of Scotland were known to the Romans as the Votadini and the Caledonians. The Romans also referred to the Caledonians as the Picts – which means 'painted people'. It could be that these were the sort of Celts who liked charging into battle naked except for a few tattoos painted on their bodies.

Agricola got a taste of the Scottish battle charge when he took on the Caledonians at a place called Mons Graupius in 84 AD. Exactly where the battle took place is not known, but it was somewhere in the north-east of the country – probably in the foothills of the Grampian mountains.

The leader of the Caledonians was called Calgacus. His name means 'swordsman' and before the battle he gave a great speech.

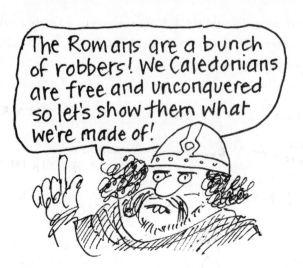

Mind you, we can't be sure what Calgacus actually said. The report of his speech was written by a Roman called Tacitus. He was Agricola's son-in-law and did not witness the events himself.

When the order to attack was given, the two sides clashed. To begin with they threw missiles at each other. Then they got up close and personal. The Caledonians swung their long, slashing swords, and the Romans stabbed with their pointy swords. Horses and chariots dashed to and fro.

According to Tacitus, the battle ended in defeat for the Caledonians, who skulked back into the hills and forests from which they had come to lick their wounds.

The truth of what happened is probably rather different to how Tacitus tells it, though. The Caledonians took a knock but they were not truly defeated. It appears they soon regrouped and started striking back at the Romans.

Things got so bad for the Romans that in order to protect themselves from the Scottish Celts they had to build not one but *two* mighty walls:

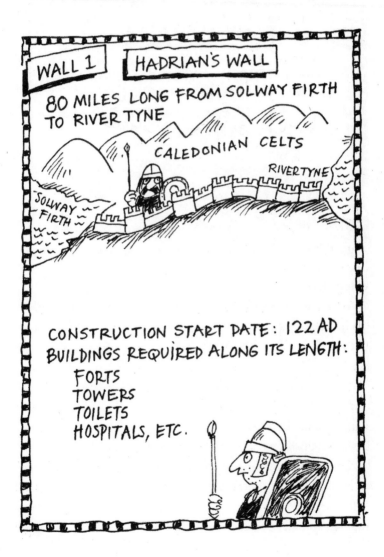

WALL 1   HADRIAN'S WALL

80 MILES LONG FROM SOLWAY FIRTH TO RIVER TYNE

CALEDONIAN CELTS

RIVER TYNE

SOLWAY FIRTH

CONSTRUCTION START DATE: 122 AD
BUILDINGS REQUIRED ALONG ITS LENGTH:
    FORTS
    TOWERS
    TOILETS
    HOSPITALS, ETC.

About twenty years later, the Romans wanted to push the boundary of the Empire north, so they built . . .

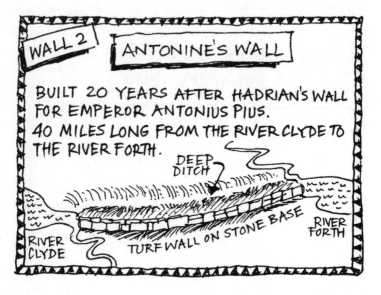

WALL 2 | ANTONINE'S WALL

BUILT 20 YEARS AFTER HADRIAN'S WALL FOR EMPEROR ANTONIUS PIUS.
40 MILES LONG FROM THE RIVER CLYDE TO THE RIVER FORTH.

DEEP DITCH

RIVER CLYDE

TURF WALL ON STONE BASE

RIVER FORTH

For almost four centuries, the Celts of southern Britain had to put up with the Romans until eventually the conquerors were forced to leave around 410 AD. And why did they leave? Well, basically the Roman Empire collapsed. It was pulled apart by squabbling politicians and rebellions from the inside, and attacks from the outside – especially by increasingly powerful Germanic tribes.

Here's an odd thing, though. For all the time the Romans had spent battling their way around the British Isles, they hardly touched the island of Ireland. Yet the Romans still had a very big impact on the Celts living there.

How so? Well, the answer has a lot to do with magic and superstition . . .

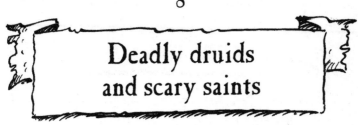

8

Deadly druids and scary saints

During the last century of Roman rule, Britain was visited by hordes of pirates looking for loot.

Often the pirates came from Ireland. As Roman power began to crumble, the raiders were tempted to come back more often.

The raiders took home treasure and slaves. Female slaves were valuable because apparently one could be exchanged in return for three dairy cows!

The pirates also took something from Britain that changed Celtic Ireland forever: Christianity. This was a new religion which had spread from the eastern Roman Empire to the Celts of Britain.

According to one famous story, Ireland actually became a Christian country as a result of pirates kidnapping a British teenage boy around the year 400 AD. The boy was called Patrick.

For six years Patrick was put to work as a shepherd in Ireland until one day he was visited by a Christian angel. The angel told Patrick to walk two hundred miles back to the coast, where a boat was waiting for him.

The boat took Patrick, along with its cargo of hunting dogs, past Britain to Gaul. Patrick didn't like Gaul much so he fled. He managed to return home to Britain, where his family were delighted to have him back.

It wasn't long, however, before the angels decided to pay Patrick another visit. This time Patrick was told to return to Ireland to teach the people – pirates and all – about the Christian God. So off he went, back to Ireland, where he set about converting the people to Christianity.

There was more drama to come in Patrick's story. But before continuing with that, we need to take a look at what the Celts believed in *before* the Christians turned up.

Well, basically the Celts believed in magic. This meant the Celts were 'pagans'. The keepers of pagan magic and knowledge were pagan priests, and the most important of these priests were the druids.

Druids could be either men or women. Along with their priestly assistants, they did different jobs. Some of these jobs sound peaceful and perfectly reasonable. They collected and stored important information, for example, and gathered herbs and plants such as mistletoe to heal the sick.

Other druid jobs were horrible – deadly, even. If you were a Celtic king who was no longer up to the job, for instance, you might find yourself being killed in the most gruesome way.

These grisly killings were known as human sacrifice. In some cases a druid watched over the sacrifice while the actual killing was done by an assistant, known as an ovate.

Other victims of sacrifice included prisoners, criminals and sometimes innocent children. It has even been suggested that druids and their worshippers may have eaten the bodies of their victims – making them Celtic cannibals!

According to some reports, Celtic priests sacrificed people to keep their gods happy. The gods worshipped by Celts included:

BRAN, THE MIGHTY GIANT.

LUGH, THE WARRIOR WITH A MAGICAL SPEAR.

OGMA, THE INVENTOR OF 'OGHAM', A WRITTEN CELTIC LANGUAGE OFTEN CARVED ONTO STONE.

Another important assistant druid was the bard, or fili. A bard's duties included telling exciting stories and reciting beautiful poetry – which all sounds rather nice. On the other hand, poetry could be deadly.

If a druid or a bard wanted to harm a person, or even an animal, they could *rhyme* them to death. The ancient Celts believed that singing a nasty song or poem could make the victim's face become all blotchy and – if the song was extra super nasty – even kill them.

Singing a death song was a way of casting a spell. When a druid wanted to cast a spell, he or she would often stand on one leg with their arms outstretched and one eye closed – like a zombie, or a strange bird.

Druids even went onto the battlefield to cast spells. Famous druid war spells included:

Speaking of warm hugs, druids were also fond of concocting love potions. These were charms that could either bring a couple together, or keep them apart.

Druids also led the people of a Celtic tribe in celebration on important holy days in the Celtic calendar. The special celebration days included:

SAMHAIN FESTIVAL HELD ON THE NIGHT OF 31ST OCTOBER (CELTIC NEW YEAR). THIS WAS THE END OF THE HARVEST SEASON. GROWING THINGS WERE CUT DOWN TO DIE. SPIRITS ROSE UP FROM THE DEAD TO PLAY TRICKS ON THE LIVING. MODERN DAY GUISING AT HALLOWE'EN PROBABLY COMES FROM THIS.

BELTANE CELTS GATHERED TO CELEBRATE THE COMING OF SUMMER BY LIGHTING FIRES ON 1ST MAY. DRUIDS USED SACRED OAK WOOD FOR THE FIRES. PEOPLE JUMPED OVER THE FLAMES OR DROVE CATTLE BETWEEN FIRES BEFORE TAKING THEM TO SUMMER PASTURES.

For hundreds or even thousands of years, druids were the guardians of the Celtic way of life. Then that way of life began to disappear – and not just because of new Christian ideas.

Even before Christianity became popular, pagan priests had been hunted down and killed by the Roman Empire. One of the worst massacres of druids was on the Welsh island of Anglesey, which in those days was called Mona.

Many druids had fled to Anglesey after the Roman invasion of Britain. But the Roman army followed the druids to the island and, in 60 AD or thereabouts, slaughtered the lot. All the druids' sacred knowledge and magical skills were lost.

It's not as if the Roman Empire actually preferred Christianity much. In the early days the Romans executed Christians – including Jesus Christ himself. But by the fourth century AD things had changed, and there were a large number of Christians living freely in the Roman Empire.

Early Christianity was actually very similar to pagan magic, which is probably why pagans were prepared to give it a try. Mind you, some pagans needed serious persuading.

When Patrick went back to Ireland, for example, he made some exceedingly brutal human sacrifices to get his message across. In a fortress by the Hill of Tara, which was the capital of ancient Ireland, Patrick tried to persuade a pagan king called Lóegaire to become Christian.

When Lóegaire refused and set druid priests on him, Patrick summoned the power of God. One of the druids was flipped high in the air and brought down so his skull smashed on a rock.

Later, the other druid tried his luck. Patrick again used the force of God and the druid was engulfed in flames.

On other occasions, there was no need for Christian preachers to resort to violence. According to one famous legend, a young Irish female druid named Brigid was taught peacefully about God and decided she would become a Christian too.

Brigid went on to build a church in a place called Kildare – or Cill Dara. Cill Dara is Irish for 'Church of the Oak', which shows that Brigid still had a pagan belief that the oak tree was sacred.

Patrick and Brigid were followed by other Christian preachers. Some of them left Ireland and went over to Britain because pagan beliefs were still strong in many places there, including Scotland and Cornwall. The Christians wanted to stamp out these beliefs and destroy any remaining druids.

The Christian missionaries had a lot to contend with along the way – not least the stormy seas around Ireland. They used incredible boats called currachs, which were made of animal hides stretched over a wooden frame.

One of these seafarers was called Columba. In the year 563 he took a stormy voyage from Ireland to Scotland, where he set about converting pagan Picts to Christianity. Along the way Columba had to battle monsters, devils and deadly druids. You can read more about his adventures in *Columba And All That*.

Another memorable missionary was Piran. According to legend, Piran didn't have the luxury of a boat when he left Ireland. A gang of kings who were jealous of Piran's Christian powers chained a millstone around his neck and then rolled him off a cliff into the sea.

Thanks to the power of God, though, Piran floated harmlessly across the waves to Cornwall, where he lived alone as a hermit. His best friends were a collection of animals, including a wolf, a badger and a bear.

Eventually news spread of Piran's special powers, and people came from far and wide to see him and become Christians.

For their efforts in destroying the pagan druids and spreading the Word of God, missionaries like Patrick, Brigit, Columba and Piran were turned into saints by the Christian Church after their death.

The legends told about their lives are partly true and partly mythical – which means untrue, unless you believe in magic and miracles. Christians prayed to these saints and regarded their bones as sacred holy relics, often collecting them in caskets.

The switch from pagan beliefs to Christian beliefs tells us a lot about how the Celtic way of life changed over the centuries. As we have discovered, some pagan beliefs survived and pagan Celtic art was transformed into the religious art of the early Christians – such as the Celtic cross.

On the other hand, the destruction of the druids meant that a vital part of Celtic life in Britain and Ireland was lost for good. Unfortunately, things would get worse before they got better . . .

9

Living legends

Our exploration of the Celts is almost at an end. It's time to recap what we've learned so far, throw in a few more details, and get to the climax of this epic story.

The ancient Celts were a fierce, smart and powerful people who once upon a time could be found living all over Europe. They had homelands in Austria and Germany, Slovakia, northern Italy, France, the British Isles, Ireland and many other places besides.

Celts were even found as far and wide as Turkey and Spain – where they were known as Celtiberians.

Then everything changed. The Celts were hunted, trapped, bashed and skewered by a range of enemy peoples – especially the Romans. The survivors were either chased away or forced to change. Many became less Celtic, and many others stopped being Celtic altogether.

Then along came the Christians, who altered the Celts' lives still further – even in places such as Ireland and Scotland, which the Romans had failed to conquer.

Couldn't everyone just leave the Celts alone for a change?

Well, no, they couldn't. At the same time as Christianity was rising from the ruins of the Roman Empire, the last Celts were attacked yet again by waves of new invaders.

In Gaul, the old Celtic way of life had already been virtually wiped out by the Romans. Now, during the fifth century, barbarian hordes turned up to steal property, conquer territory and stamp out any last traces of Celticness. These barbarians included:

In Britain and Ireland, many people clung on to their old Celtic way of life – especially in the west and north. But now fresh conquerors arrived from mainland Europe. These were the Anglo-Saxons, followed later by the Vikings and the Normans.

The Anglo-Saxons took over England and then tried to do the same in Scotland. Some Anglo-Saxons – or Angles, to be precise – moved into the south-eastern corner of Scotland. But you might remember they were severely thumped at the Battle of Dun Nechtain in 685 AD. Those Angles who stuck around eventually joined with the Celts to become Scots.

Meanwhile, Celts in Wales and Cornwall were also attacked by the Anglo-Saxons. The pressure took its toll. A lot of Celts from these areas fled over the water to Brittany, which was the last refuge of the Celts in Gaul.

Then the Welsh and Cornish Celts fought back, winning a series of bloody battles to stop the Anglo-Saxons from completely taking over.

But there was more mayhem to come. At the end of the eighth century, the Vikings turned up. These wild Scandinavian raiders piled in to fight both the Celts *and* the Anglo-Saxons.

In the midst of all this chaos, at least one positive thing happened. Many of the invaders eventually settled down peacefully and the modern nations we know today as England, Ireland, Scotland and Wales began to take shape.

The last big disaster for the Celts was probably the invasion of the Normans, who came from Normandy in France. In 1066, an army of Normans turned up at Hastings on England's south coast and won a famous battle, seizing control of the kingdom. Mind you, by that time England was more Anglo-Saxon than Celtic anyway.

After taking over England, the Normans eventually blended with the Anglo-Saxons to become Anglo-Normans. Together they set their sights on conquering the remaining Celtic countries on their doorstep.

In Wales a brave and beautiful Celtic princess called

Gwenllian ferch Gruffydd helped inspire a rebellion against the Anglo-Normans in 1136. But Gwenllian was captured in battle and beheaded, and in later years the Welsh Celts were eventually conquered.

Meanwhile, the last Celtic kings of Scotland and Ireland were defeated or forced to change to Anglo-Norman ways.

Thanks to the Normans and Anglo-Saxons, it looked like the last of the Celts were crushed once and for all. In other words the Celts were dead. Buried. Finished. End of. (You get the idea.)

Except that's only partly true. Yes, the people of Britain and Ireland no longer had most of the beliefs and traditions of the ancient Celts. But they still felt a strong connection with their Celtic past. Many continued to speak Celtic languages and make Celtic art, for example.

People still believed in pagan magic, too, although this could be dangerous. Those who cast magic spells could find themselves being accused of witchcraft and even burned at the stake!

There was a much less dangerous way to remember your Celtic roots, though. This was to tell stories. Preferably the stories were exciting legends with lots of romance, action and adventure. Luckily, there were still Celtic bards around whose storytelling skills brought legends to life.

One of the most popular legends of medieval times was about Arthur. He was believed to have been a brave and skilful Celtic warrior king who defended the Celts of Britain against the invading Anglo-Saxons.

There may have been a King Arthur in real life but nobody knows for sure. Some bits of the stories about him are probably based on facts – meaning things that really happened – but mostly they are myth. Just in case you are wondering, a myth is an imaginary story and a legend is a story that combines myths and facts.

The legend of Arthur has been told in many different ways. It begins something like this:

THE QUEEN GAVE BIRTH TO A BOY CALLED ARTHUR. TRUE TO HIS WORD, THE KING RELUCTANTLY GAVE THE BABY TO THE WIZARD.

THE WIZARD WAS CALLED MERLIN AND WAS ACTUALLY GOOD AND KIND. HE TOOK ARTHUR TO A NOBLEMAN'S CASTLE TO BE BROUGHT UP THERE.

ARTHUR GREW UP NOT KNOWING HIS REAL PARENTS OR THAT HE HAD ROYAL BLOOD.

WHEN ARTHUR'S DAD DIED THE KINGDOM WAS LEFT WITHOUT AN HEIR TO THE THRONE. NOBLEMEN SQUABBLED AMONG THEMSELVES OVER WHO SHOULD BE THE NEXT RULER.

MERLIN DECIDED TO SORT OUT THE MESS. HE CAST A SPELL AND A BOULDER APPEARED WITH A SWORD STUCK IN IT.

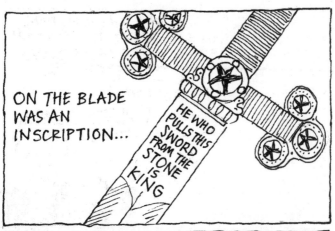

ON THE BLADE WAS AN INSCRIPTION...

HE WHO PULLS THIS SWORD FROM THE STONE IS KING

BEFORE LONG, THE RIVAL NOBLES TURNED UP AND CROWDED ROUND THE STONE.

ONE BY ONE THEY TRIED TO PULL THE SWORD FROM THE ROCK BUT IT WOULDN'T BUDGE.

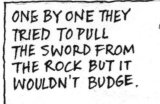

WHEN ARTHUR WAS FIFTEEN, HE WAS TAKEN TO THE SWORD IN THE STONE. HE PUT HIS HAND ON THE SWORD...

...AND CAREFULLY PULLED IT OUT.

WHEN PEOPLE DISCOVERED WHAT HAD HAPPENED, ARTHUR WAS CROWNED KING.

As he grew into a man, Arthur defended his kingdom heroically against Anglo-Saxon invaders. He married a lady called Guinevere who became his queen. With Merlin at his side and a band of brave knights, including Sir Lancelot and Sir Galahad, Arthur had many adventures.

Nobody knows exactly how or when the story of Arthur first appeared. We do know that Arthur was mentioned in a Welsh poem called 'Y Gododdin', which might have been composed at the end of the sixth century.

Around that time, Welsh-speaking Celts actually had kingdoms in northern England and southern Scotland – all battling the invading Angles. So a heroic king with a magical sword would have been very popular!

There are lots of places around Britain named after Arthur. The map on the next page shows some examples.

Arthur is only one of the many great Celtic legends passed down through the ages. Another medieval story popular in Ireland and Scotland was the legend of a boy called Cú Chulainn – which is pronounced 'Coo-hullin'.

Cú Chulainn was a young warrior with magical powers who lived in Ulster in the north of Ireland. He was handsome, brave and kind. But woe betide anyone who made him angry.

In battle Cú Chulainn would jump off his chariot to hack off his enemies' heads, and if he got really mad he would transform into a hideous, terrifying monster.

Speaking of monsters, Cú Chulainn had a companion called the Morrigan. The Morrigan was a 'shapeshifter' who could change from a beautiful girl into a wolf, and was not to be messed with!

ARTHUR'S SEAT — A FAMOUS HILL IN SCOTLAND'S CAPITAL CITY — EDINBURGH.

IT'S SAID THAT THE ENGLISH CITY OF CARLISLE IS ONE OF THE PLACES WHERE ARTHUR HELD COURT.

NEAR SWANSEA IN WALES THERE'S A MYSTERIOUS BOULDER CALLED ARTHUR'S STONE.

THERE'S A CLIFF IN WALES CALLED CRAIG Y DDINAS. IT'S SAID THERE'S A SECRET CAVE UNDER IT WHERE ARTHUR AND HIS KNIGHTS LIE SLEEPING.

I feel just a little bit peckish!

Nowadays, incredible legends and exciting real history are the things that keep people interested in the Celts. Since the 1800s we have university professors of all things Celtic, Celtic language lessons at school and modern druids (they don't do human sacrifice any more, though).

People are still inspired by the Celts to make art, poetry, books and films – especially fantasy books and films. You know the sort of thing – filled with kind-hearted heroes, powerful enemies, magical weapons, strange beasts, mysterious wizards, terrifying rituals and great adventures. These stories often borrow the language, clothes and artwork of the ancient Celts too.

Perhaps you have an idea for a story of your own, inspired by everything you've learned about the ancient Celts? If so, it's time to start writing down your ideas . . .

Timeline

700 BC	The Celts appear around this time and start using iron
390 BC	Celtic warrior Brennus attacks Rome
279 BC	Another Brennus attacks Greece
58 BC	Romans invade Gaul and Vercingetorix leads a doomed rebellion
55 BC	First Roman attack on Celtic Britain
43 AD	Romans invade Britain – and this time they're here to stay
60 AD	British Celtic princess Boudicca leads a doomed rebellion against the Romans
84 AD	Celts of Scotland (the Caledonians) fight Romans at Battle of Mons Graupius
122–142 AD	Hadrian's Wall and Antonine's Wall built to keep Scottish Celts out of Roman Britain
400 AD	Patrick is kidnapped by pirates and later becomes a Christian preacher in Ireland
410 AD	The Roman Empire collapses and the Roman army leaves Britain

450 AD	Anglo-Saxons invade Britain around this time and some Celts flee to Brittany
563 AD	Columba sails from Ireland to Scotland and battles Celtic druids using Christian miracles
c.600 AD	The legendary King Arthur is mentioned in 'Y Gododdin', a Welsh poem
685 AD	Scottish Celts (the Picts) destroy an invading Anglo-Saxon army
c.790 AD	Vikings attack Britain, causing mayhem for both Celts and Anglo-Saxons
1066 AD	Normans conquer Anglo-Saxon England and threaten Celts of Wales, Scotland and Ireland
1136 AD	Princess Gwenllian of Wales leads doomed rebellion against the Normans
1000–1400 AD	Last Celtic rulers of Scotland, Wales and Ireland
1660 AD	Celtic expert Edward Lhuyd is born in Wales
1877 AD	First professor of Celtic at Oxford University
1882 AD	First professor of Celtic at Edinburgh University